MASTERING DEEP POINT OF VIEW

Simple steps to make your stories irresistible to your readers

---

ALICE GAINES

Writer's Fun Zone Publishing

Published by Writer's Fun Zone Publishing, 771 Kingston
Ave., Suite 108, Piedmont, California 94611

Cover by Ezra Barany.

Editing and book production by Beth Barany.

ISBN Print: 978-1-944841-19-5 (1st edition)

ISBN E-book: 978-1-944841-20-1 (1st edition)

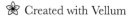 Created with Vellum

Contents

Preface

When I first read Alice's article on creating deep point of view in an anthology, I was editing for our romance writing community, I was impressed by how these simple techniques could create a closeness with the reader. I knew immediately that I wanted to share it with as many fiction writers as possible.

Now, I'm excited to bring Alice's techniques on mastering deep point of view to you.

~Beth Barany, Editor and Publisher

What This Book Covers

WHAT IF YOU could master a simple technique to make your stories irresistible to your readers?

Even if your prose is beautiful, your characters feel alive, and your plot twists and turns, you can still get one-star reviews complaining that your story didn't grab readers. There's a technique that will help your readers fall in love with your characters, so they feel your characters' emotions as the story unfolds. It is called Deep Point of View (POV) and is a powerful tool for pulling readers into your story.

I don't want readers saying that they just couldn't get into your story or that they didn't care about your characters enough to keep reading. So, if you want to write your story so that your readers just can't put your book down, take advantage of deep point of view.

When you use the techniques of deep point

of view, your readers:

- experience the story through your characters' eyes
- are immersed in the story world, seeing it more vividly
- care more about your characters, so they care more about your story.

In other words, by implementing the tools I share in this book, you'll master a key craft technique of showing versus telling.

In this book, you'll learn:

- what deep point of view is and how you can access it
- how to spot the distancing language that creates a barrier between the story and your reader
- three language tools to bring the reader right into the story and into your characters
- why you may not want to always use deep point of view

This book will give you specific tools for mastering deep point of view. You'll learn how to spot when you're using distancing language and slipping out of deep point of view. I hope this book will help you master these tools to create intimacy between your story and your reader.

I first taught this material in a few workshops and then in a webinar training sponsored by Beth Barany and her online school for fiction writers, Barany School of Fiction. Beth asked if I'd like to make this work more accessible and bring it to you in book form.

To support you in applying what I teach about deep point of view, we have created some worksheets for you. Whether you're reading in print or e-book format, you can go here to grab those handouts:

http://bethb.net/deeppovbook.

WHO THIS BOOK IS FOR

This book was written for writers of genre fiction, such as romance, mystery, horror, thriller, etc. who want to understand deep point of view and integrate it into their prose, either in the writing or in the editing phase. The point of view tools shared here can also be applied to any other styles of fiction writing.

ABOUT ALICE GAINES

I wasn't always a writer. In fact, my background is not in literature. I didn't get along with my high school English teacher. Needless to say,

English was not my favorite subject. I didn't get the best grades in it at all. My academic background is in Psychology and I have a Ph.D. in Personality Psychology from the University of California at Berkeley. I use psychology in my writing and will describe how the study of psychology can apply to your writing.

The other major part of my background I use in my writing is acting. I studied acting for many years. While I was never a professional actor, I started acting when I was in junior high, stuck with it through college, many years ago. As I write, I tend to get myself into my point of view character's head, put myself in the scene, and look around at what's going on. Then I start acting and notice what other people are doing in the scene. Yeah. It's crazy. (Though I think you can relate, if you're reading this book!)

While I don't have direct experience writing other genres—I am a romance novelist—my feeling is the tools I'm offering on deep point of view will work in other genres. Give them a try and let me know.

BIASES ABOUT POINT OF VIEW

I'm a point of view purist. I prefer to be in one point of view per scene. I want to get into one head, and I don't want to be pulled out of that head until the scene changes and something else happens. That preference is not universal. Many people switch points of view in the middle of a scene. If you do it well, I'll enjoy it as a reader and keep reading. But if it's distracting and pulls me out of the story, I may not finish your book. Good point of view is what really gets me into a story.

That being said, keep this quote in mind:

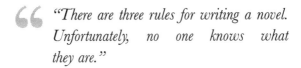

"There are three rules for writing a novel. Unfortunately, no one knows what they are."

—W. Somerset Maugham

Take what's useful from this book and leave the rest.

ON POINT OF VIEW

Since I only cover deep point of view in this book, you may want a reference that gives you a good overview of the entire range of point of view. I recommend Alicia Rasley's excellent book on point of view, *The Power of Point of View.* She includes first-person, second-person, third-person, and omniscient. What I discuss in this book, she covers in Chapter 10 and calls it "deep immersion." (More references are listed in the Resources section at the end of this book.)

What is Deep Point of View?

I FIRST GOT into this subject when I wrote an article for my Romance Writers of America chapter's anthology about writing romance called "Getting the Author Off the Page," sometimes called author intrusion. (The anthology is *Writing Romance: The Ultimate Guide on Craft, Creation and Industry Connections*.)

Later, I came to realize that what people were calling deep point of view was really about getting rid of this author intrusion, or getting the author off the page. I decided to go to my friend, the Google machine, and see what people were saying about deep point of view.

Here's a quote about deep point of view I agree with:

"Deep point of view is intense. It not only represents the sights, sounds, and actions filtered through a POV (point of view) character but goes deeper into emotions as well as a character's unique worldview. In deep point of view the character owns the page and the author becomes nonexistent. Deep point of view allows the reader to live vicariously through the actions, reactions, and emotions of a character."

Rhay Christou, writing teacher and member of Maggie Lawson's Writer's Academy

PROBLEMS WHEN NOT USING DEEP POV

You may not want to use deep point of view in your story, but some problems can arise when you don't.

For example, you may not engage the reader when you don't provide them with an experience. Using explanations and relaying information doesn't necessarily make for a good story, to paraphrase from author/editor, Genevieve Iseult Eldredge.

In the coming sections, we'll see problems—things we do that we are unaware of—that, unfortunately, end up telling rather than showing the story.

What are the signs of telling and not showing?

" Events and characters' emotions are simply reported to the reader [and] "...The point of view is distant. We never get inside the character's mind. We never find out what they're thinking or why..."

Genevieve Iseult Eldredge

Too much telling and not showing is a good reason for getting your manuscript rejected, at least in a romance house.

WHAT EXACTLY IS DEEP POINT OF VIEW?

Essentially, deep point of view allows the reader to live vicariously through the actions, reactions, and emotions of a character, the "point of view" character. (Source: Rhay Christou)

The point of view character isn't always the

main character. In romance, we tend to have two main characters. I usually think of the woman as the protagonist, and the male as the other protagonist. Generally, you can go from the female point of view in one scene to the male point of view in another scene, and so on. In other genres, mystery or thriller for example, you want to use the killer's point of view as well as the detective's point of view.

WHY DEEP POV IS USEFUL

Readers want to feel as if they are in your story. They want to be transported to a new world. When you skillfully use the tools of deep point of view, you make it easy for the reader to slip into the heart, mind, body, and soul of your point of view-character, most often your main character.

Deep point of view creates an intimacy that other levels of point of view do not. Deep point of view is a choice and may not always be the right one for every moment. Consider the type of story you're writing and if you may want a filter between the point of view character and the reader.

Many times, when people discuss deep point of view, they will talk about things like filtering or distancing words that keep the character separated from the reader. In this book, we'll be very specific about what kinds of words can be filtering or distancing.

How to Access Deep POV

BEFORE YOU CAN WRITE in deep point of view, you need to be able to access your point of view character from the inside. You need to get into your character's heart, mind, body, and soul.

There are several ways to do this.

One way to do this is role-playing. Prepare the character as an actor would, and then crawl into her skin.

That's what I do. I know my character. I get into my character. I know what the situation is. I know what the conflict in the scene is, who the other people in the room are, and I get in there and I start writing.

Other people will do things like character descriptions and interviews, learning every aspect of the character from her likes and her dislikes, her personal history, how she talks, how she moves, people she loves and hates, etc.

Writers who like to do a lot of preparation before they actually start writing will do extensive character interviews, descriptions, and journal entries.

Of course, you can do both of these things: role playing and doing character sketches and interviews. They're not mutually exclusive. They're just different ways of getting into character.

Even if you do all your homework, you can still get into trouble with distancing and filtering words as you write. In the next section, I'll explain these distancing and filtering words in detail.

To help get you into your point of view character, here's a role-playing exercise adapted from Alicia Rasley's book, *The Power of Point of View*.

EXERCISE

To get deeply into your character's point of view, close your eyes for a moment and put yourself in this character's mind. Then open your eyes and write to this prompt, "What's happening, *character name*?"

Answer in the first-person.

Don't worry if it doesn't come out easily. Don't stop to edit. Just write in the "I" mode until the character, or your subconscious, takes over.

Now review what you wrote in that first-person voice and translate into the third-person. Often this will be already deep point of view.

EXAMPLE: FIRST-PERSON

I'm lying in a darkened room. One I've never seen before. No, wait, maybe I have. Last night?

I ease my legs over the side of the bed, and my head spins as I sit up. I'm naked except for a man's shirt. Have I seen this shirt before? Did I put it on?

My stomach is churning, and my head feels full of cotton balls. How many drinks did I have last night? I remember the beer, and then someone had opened a bottle of tequila. Poison. I should never drink the stuff.

The door opens, and a man walks in. Bare-chested. I'm wearing his shirt. He pulls back the curtains from the window, and sunlight pours in. I cringe and squeeze my eyes shut.

"Morning, sunshine," he says. Way too cheerful.

EXAMPLE: THIRD-PERSON

She was lying in a darkened room—one she'd

never seen before. No, wait, maybe she had. Could it have been last night?

She eased her legs over the side of the bed, and as she sat up, her head seemed to spin on her shoulders. Oh, crap. She was naked except for a man's shirt, so big she swam in it. She lifted the tails. Had she seen this shirt before? Maybe she'd put it on. Nothing from the previous night came through clearly.

Her stomach churned. Not a good sign. And her head seemed full of cotton balls. How many drinks had she had the night before? The beer. And then someone had opened a bottle of tequila. She never drank that stuff. It was poison.

The door opened, and a man entered. Bare-chested. The owner of the shirt? He pulled back the curtains from the windows, and sunlight poured in. She cringed and squeezed her eyes shut.

"Morning, sunshine," he said. Way too cheerful under the circumstances.

Part 1: The 3 Tools to Craft Deep POV

Tool #1: These Verbs Aren't Your Friend

THE FOLLOWING KINDS of verbs put distance or a filter between the story and your reader. Watch out for these in your manuscript, so that you can delete them and replace them with stronger language. I'll show you how as we go through each of them. The types of verbs are:

- Perceiving verbs
- Thinking verbs
- Emoting verbs

If you're using these types of verbs, you're running the risk of "telling" the reader what's going on, versus allowing them to experience it, i.e., "showing."

Let's dive in.

DELETE AND REPLACE PERCEIVING VERBS

What are "perceiving verbs"?

They are verbs expressing any of the five senses—these verbs and similar ones:

- To see
- To hear
- To taste
- To feel
- To smell
- To notice, etc.

When you're editing, delete and replace the perceiving verbs. I'll show you what I mean in the examples below. In these examples, Kelly is the point of view character.

EXAMPLE 1

Kelly heard her phone ring.

When you cut the perceiving verb "heard," you can rewrite the sentence like this:

The phone rang.

We've cut both the verb "heard" (the perceiving verb) and "Kelly" (the subject). We already know that Kelly is doing the perceiving.

HERE'S ANOTHER EXAMPLE.

EXAMPLE 2
She felt the satin under her fingers.

When you cut the perceiving verb "felt" and, since we know the point of view character is doing the feeling, you can rewrite the sentence like this:

She ran her fingertips over the satin.
OR
The satin was smooth under her fingertips.

IN THE FIRST REWRITTEN EXAMPLE, we have the subject "she" and an action "ran." The reader will automatically put herself in the subject's place and fill in the blanks about what it's like to run one's fingertips over the satin.

In the second rewritten example, the reader gets an experience as if they are Kelly, experiencing the satin for themselves.

YOUR TURN

Delete and replace the perceiving verbs. Your answer does not have to have the word "Kelly" in it. As a matter of fact, it very likely won't. We want to get rid of "saw" because we're not going to tell the reader what Kelly is seeing, we're going to let the reader see it through Kelly's eyes.

EXERCISE 1
Kelly saw a flash of light.

Possible replacements:
A flash of light blinded Kelly.
A flash of light blinded her.
Light flashed.
The flash of light was blinding.
There was a flash of light.
Lightning struck. (This is a good one. Now we know exactly what kind of light it was.)
She caught a flash of light out of the corner of her eye.
A flash of light drew him away from the purse.

EXERCISE 2
Kelly was cold.

Possible replacements:

She shivered.

She shivered in her jacket.

Kelly shivered from the chilled air.

An icy chill ran across her shoulders.

The frigid breeze made her skin pebble.

A chill wind bit the back of her neck.

Goosebumps rose on her skin.

The cold breeze quickly lowered her body temperature. She shivered.

DELETE AND REPLACE: THINKING VERBS

What are "thinking verbs"?

These verbs and similar ones:

- To know
- To wonder
- To think
- To doubt
- To question
- To realize
- To imagine/ponder/muse
- To be puzzled or confused, etc.

EXAMPLE 1

She questioned his motives.

When you cut the thinking verb "questioned," you can rewrite the sentence like this:

He was up to no good. He wasn't doing this for her benefit, so why was he?

People generally know when they're questioning somebody else's motives, but what is going on in their head at the time? It's going to be something like, "He was up to no good. He wasn't doing this for her benefit, so why was he?" That's what it sounds like in your head when you're questioning someone else's motives.

EXAMPLE 2
What, she wondered, was he thinking?

When you cut the thinking verb "wondered," you can rewrite the sentence like this:

What was he thinking?

We see this in romance all the time. The "she wondered," is just a filter word. That's just the author telling me that whoever the point of view character is, maybe it's Kelly, is wondering about something. Just take it out. "What was he thinking?"

If you want more information about how

she feels about the guy, then write: "What in the hell was he thinking?" or "What was the stubborn man thinking?"

EXAMPLE 3

She realized she was in the wrong room.

When you cut the thinking verb "realized," you can rewrite the sentence like this:

She was in the wrong room.
OR
Hell, she was in the wrong room.

You can state simply: "She was in the wrong room." Or, if you want to portray how she feels about being in the wrong room: "Hell, she was in the wrong room." Maybe she happened on something she wasn't supposed to see? Or maybe she's made herself late for a job interview.

YOUR TURN

Delete and replace the thinking verbs. As with the previous exercises, your answer does not have to have the word Kelly in it. As a matter of fact, it very likely won't.

EXERCISE 1

Kelly wondered if it was going to rain.

Possible replacements:

Was it going to rain?

The pewter clouds threatened to rain

If the rain came this afternoon, all my work would be for naught.

Shit. Rain was coming.

The dark clouds threatened rain. The clouds threatened rain.

The air was heavy with ozone. She'd better grab her umbrella.

Moisture hung in the air. Was it going to rain?

EXERCISE 2

Kelly knew he was a smart man.

Possible replacements:

He was a smart man.

Surely, he knew better than this.

Ain't no moss growing on his head.

His eyes radiated intelligence.

He had a PhD, for God's sake. Why couldn't he figure this out?

With his $10 words, he knew his stuff.

I had no doubt of his intelligence, but could I trust him?

Smart guy. He wasn't going to be fooled easily.

He knew all the answers.

His sly smile indicated otherwise.

DELETE AND REPLACE: EMOTING VERBS

What are emoting verbs?

These verbs and similar ones:

- To love, hate, like, desire, fear, dread, mourn, wish, etc.
- To feel anger, hope, fear, joy, sadness or any other emotion

Let's dive into our examples and show how to you can replace emoting verbs to create deep point of view.

EXAMPLE 1

She hated snakes, and there was one not six inches from her foot.

When you cut the emoting verb "hated," you can rewrite the sentence like this:

Snakes. Oh, God. Slithery monsters with fangs. And there was one not six inches from her foot.

I love snakes, but lots of people really hate

27

snakes. If you hate snakes, and there's one six inches away from you, do you sit there and think: "I hate snakes."? No, it's more likely you'd think: "Snakes, oh my God. Slithery monsters with fangs, and there is one not six inches from my foot." You might only say an exclamation like, "Snakes? Oh my God!" Your immediate reaction is not going to be, "Oh, yeah. I really hate snakes."

EXAMPLE 2
Fury coursed through him.

When you cut the emoting verb "coursed," you can rewrite the sentence like this:

Blasted barnacles!

We hear this a lot. In other words, "I'm furious," or "I'm angry." What goes on in your head when fury is coursing through you? I know what goes on in my head when I'm driving along on the freeway and somebody cuts me off. I don't think, "I'm really furious at that guy." I think, "That idiot cut me off."

As I said at the beginning, there are no rules; it's about what works. So, "Fury coursed through him," could work, but I recommend you follow it up with all the other things, like: "Fury coursed through me. The idiot had just cut me off, and I'm going 70 miles an hour on the freeway."

EXAMPLE 3
Kelly hated sauerkraut.

When you cut the emoting verb "hated," you can rewrite the sentence like this:

He'd loaded her hot dog with grody sauerkraut.
OR
Ugh, sauerkraut.

What do you think, what do you feel, what goes on inside you, when you're confronted by a bunch of sauerkraut? Well, you might just say, "He loaded my hot dog with grody sauerkraut," or simply, "Yuck, sauerkraut."

YOUR TURN

Delete and replace the emoting verbs. To answer this, you'll need to figure out what Kelly is afraid of (or sad about, or what she hopes for), and confront her with that.

EXERCISE 1
Fear gripped Kelly.

Possible replacements:

Her body froze. She couldn't move.

The snake wrapped around her ankle.

I had to force stillness on my shaking hands.

She froze.

Her mouth dry, she pressed her trembling knee against the counter.

She froze, speechless.

She bit back a scream.

Oh, God. It's 300 feet.

A scream welled up in her throat.

EXERCISE 2

Losing her dog broke Kelly's heart.

Possible replacements:

Pain lanced her heart. Her dog was gone.

Unable to concentrate, all I could think of was my little lost dog. Would I ever see her again?

"He's gone," she sobbed. "I'll never give my love away to another mutt again."

The leash dangled in her hand. No more walks.

The tears fell. The hurt, unbearable.

It wasn't the same without Boots to warm her belly.

Kelly held her dog's limp paw in her hand and stared at the lifeless body, the tears soaking Spirit's soft, brown coat.

Kelly stayed in the bed's softness all night in the dark, unable to be alone.

EXERCISE 3

Kelly hoped it would be George on the phone.

Possible replacements:
Oh, God, could it be George calling?
Please let that be George Clooney calling.
That had better be George on the phone.
It was George.
Would George call so soon?
The phone rang, and my heart leaped. It had to be George.

LET'S REVIEW: PERCEIVING VERBS

EXAMPLE
Perceiving verb: to see

She saw a rider approaching her down the path between the trees. As he drew nearer, she noticed a look of fury on his face.

Cut the perceiving verbs "saw" and "noticed" and change the sentence to:

A rider approached along the path between the trees, a light of fury gleaming in his eyes.

EXAMPLE

Perceiving verb: to smell

When she opened the box, she smelled something foul.

Cut the perceiving verb "smelled" and change the sentence to:

When she opened the box, the contents gave off a foul odor.

EXAMPLE
Perceiving verb: to feel/touch

She felt the silk of the dress whisper over her body.

Cut the perceiving verb "felt" and change the sentence to:

The silk of the dress whispered over her body.

LET'S REVIEW: THINKING VERBS

EXAMPLE
Thinking verb: to be confused

The recipe confused her.

Cut the thinking verb "confused," and change the sentence to:

Was it three cups of sugar or four?

EXAMPLE
Thinking verb: to realize

She realized she'd failed.

Cut the thinking verb "realized" and change the sentence to:

Damn, failure. And she'd tried so hard.

LET'S REVIEW: EMOTING VERBS

EXAMPLE 1 (From Rhay Christou)
Emoting verb: to feel

He felt the pain shoot through his gut and wondered if he was going to die.

In the rewritten sentence, also by Rhay Christou, we're shown what he feels and hear his thoughts.

Pain shot through his gut, and he clutched his stomach. This was it. He was going to die.

"With the first sentence, the reader is kept at a distance. He hears what the character's thoughts are, but doesn't feel what the character feels. He doesn't think what the character thinks. He is told about these feelings and thoughts, and as a result there is a filter between the reader and character."

Rhay Christou

EXAMPLE 2
Emoting verb: to wish

She wished she could offer him tea.

Cut the emoting verb "wished" and change the sentence to:

Her pitiful lodgings didn't allow her to offer him tea.
How shabby she must seem to him.

EXAMPLE 3: (From author, Kristen Kieffer)

Not in deep point of view:

"At last the tremors subsided and the earth stilled. Maggie wondered how bad the earthquake had been. She looked around and saw the deep black gashes in the ground where the pavement of the road had cracked. She knew that it must have been at least a 7.0."

In deep point of view:

"At last the earth stilled, the trembling ground sighing into complacency. How bad had this one been? Around her, wide gashes in the pavement revealed that the quake had split the road as though it were soft as flesh. Maggie shivered despite the heat. A 7.0 at least, perhaps even higher."

"SEE how the second draft removes the words "wondered," "saw," and "knew"? This allows the reader to jump inside Maggie's head, reeling with her as her town is struck by an earthquake." (Source: "How to Write in Deep Point Of View" by Kristen Kieffer)

A WORD ABOUT YOUR VIEWPOINT CHARACTER

Editor Beth Hill reminds us that "...(T)he reader knows automatically that what is being reported are the thoughts and feelings and the intentions of the viewpoint character..."

She continues:

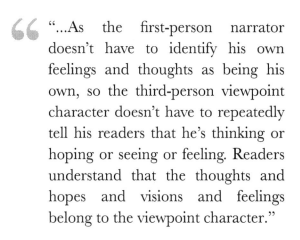 "...As the first-person narrator doesn't have to identify his own feelings and thoughts as being his own, so the third-person viewpoint character doesn't have to repeatedly tell his readers that he's thinking or hoping or seeing or feeling. Readers understand that the thoughts and hopes and visions and feelings belong to the viewpoint character."

(Source: editor Beth Hill, *The Magic of Fiction: Crafting Words into Story – The Writer's Guide to Writing and Editing*)

LET'S PRACTICE!

Let's put it all together and rewrite the following passage:

SHE SAW his gloves lying on the table where he'd left them. She'd expected him to return, but now sadness washed over her as she realized he never would.

Her maid, Sarah, entered the room, and Mary could see Sarah's unhappiness on her face. Mary knew Sarah had loved George like her own son.

"That dreadful Mr. Simms is here," Sarah said.

"Shall I send him away?"

George's solicitor. Mary couldn't stomach the man, but she knew she'd have to deal with him sooner or later. "Show him in."

"Are you sure, my lady?"

Mary rubbed the bridge of her nose between her thumb and forefinger. God, she was tired. "I'm sure."

Sarah left, and Mary steeled herself for what she felt would be an unpleasant encounter.

HERE'S one way to rewrite this in deep point of view:

HIS GLOVES LAY on the table, waiting for him to return. Just a brief trip, away for a few days, and he'd come home to her. But he wouldn't.

The tightness in her chest made breathing difficult, each intake of air painful. She'd never look at his face again nor hear his laughter.

Her maid, Sarah, entered the room, and Sarah's gaze fell on the gloves. For a moment, tears glistened at the corners of Sarah's eyes. After all, the older woman had loved George like her own son.

"That dreadful Mr. Simms is here," Sarah said. "Shall I send him away?"

George's solicitor. Distasteful fellow who employed exaggerated courtesy to mask a grasping, greedy nature. She could refuse to see him today, but she'd have to deal with him sooner or later. "Show him in."

"Are you sure, my lady?"

Mary rubbed the bridge of her nose between her thumb and forefinger. She only had to endure this interview, and then she could crawl into her bed and pull the covers over her face. "I'm sure."

Sarah left, and Mary straightened her spine.

She'd need every bit of strength she could muster for an unpleasant encounter. She'd face Simms down somehow because she had to.

YOU MAY SAY, "There's way more description and detail in the second passage." That's kind of the point.

When you're deep in a character's point of view, if you're deeply into their head, you're going to be taking in all the different details around you, all the things that impact that view. You're going to be remembering when he bought the gloves, or that he was always forgetting his gloves on that table. "He forgot his gloves again, and now I'll never be able to give them to him again." You get all the feelings. Sarah's feelings come through strongly, just through the presence of tears in her eyes, but you're not saying, *"Mary saw the tears."* No, there are tears in Sarah's eyes. You get it more directly. As Alicia Rasley says in her book, and I'm paraphrasing: we perceive in elaboration, not in summary.

In other words, when we're in the here and now, when we're in the world, we perceive things in detail. We rarely summarize our experiences to ourselves as they are happening, saying to ourselves, "I'm sad. I'm coming home again."

If you do get into deep point of view, I think you're very naturally going to use more detail, as opposed to summarizing things, like telling people what the characters are feeling or seeing or thinking.

TO REVIEW TOOL #1: VERBS THAT AREN'T YOUR FRIENDS

Here's a list of the verbs that aren't your friends. You can also download these with the handout packet here: http://bethb.net/deeppovbook.

PERCEIVING VERBS: To see, hear, taste, feel, smell, notice, etc.

THINKING VERBS: To know, wonder, think, doubt, question, realize, imagine, ponder, muse, be puzzled or confused, etc.

EMOTING VERBS: To love, hate, like, desire, fear, dread, mourn, wish, etc. or to feel anger, hope, fear, joy, sadness or any other emotion.

IF YOU LOOK at what people refer to as either distancing words or filter words, they generally fall into one of these three categories of verbs. These are the words you want to look out for in your own writing. See if you can replace them and use stronger ways of portraying what's actually going on in your point of view character's head and heart.

Tool #2: Internal Monologue Isn't Your Friend

NEXT, I'll share a tool to delete and replace "direct inner monologue."

Here's what I mean...

PROBLEM: Internal Monologue is not your friend

SOLUTION: Delete and replace direct inner monologues

LITTLE PULLS me out of a story faster and more completely than for the character suddenly to start talking to me in first-person present tense when the rest of the story is third-person past tense.

Often, in first-person present tense, direct inner monologue can interrupt the flow. Instead, use third-person indirect thought.

Here's a before-and-after example:

BEFORE EXAMPLE

The crowd around Carla seemed to buzz and
hum with a life greater than the sum of the
people in attendance. Animated conversation,
the clink of glasses, occasional laughter. All very
festive and totally foreign to her normal quiet
evenings with friends.

I just have to endure this evening, she thought. *A few
more hours and I can get the hell out of here.*

BUT INTERNAL MONOLOGUE is not your
friend. I'll explain why.

First of all, the author inserted, "she
thought," right in there, but the main point is
when I'm in the upper paragraph, which starts
with the crowd around Carla, I think I am in
her head. I think I'm getting all those things
portrayed through her senses and her feelings.
Then I get to the second paragraph and the
internal monologue in first person pulls me right
out of the story. It tells me that in the first paragraph I wasn't inside Carla's head, but now
I am.

When I started writing, I entered a lot of
contests, and I used internal monologue. Not a
lot, but I used it. Finally, one blessed contest
judge wrote something like this to me, and I will

thank her forever… "Why do you do that? You don't need to portray internal monologue in this way. Your entire story is internal monologue."

That's the whole point. We are in the character's head. We're experiencing the character's feelings directly, in real time.

As writers, we use a funny convention to show what's actually going on in the person's head. We translate it into third-person past tense. You need to be aware that even though this sounds like I'm telling a story, what I'm really doing is expressing the story as it happens directly. The story is all internal monologue.

To get rid of direct inner monologues that interrupt the flow, rewrite them. Here's what I mean, rewriting the example from above:

AFTER EXAMPLE

The crowd around Carla seemed to buzz and hum with a life greater than the sum of the people in attendance. Animated conversation, the clink of glasses, occasional laughter. All very festive and totally foreign to her normal quiet evenings with friends.
She just had to endure this evening. A few more hours and she could get the hell out of here.

I DELETED "SHE THOUGHT," changed it to third-person past tense, and eliminated the italics. Now I'm not kicked out of the story.

BEFORE

"*I just have to endure this evening,*" she thought. "*A few more hours and I can get the hell out of here.*"

AFTER

She just had to endure this evening. A few more hours and she could get the hell out of here.

A SIMPLE CHANGE that can keep the reader in the story, instead of having them bumped out.

Tool #3: The Fundamental Attribution Error

YOU NOW HAVE two direct tools: the three sets of verbs and avoiding internal monologue. These things are not your friends. I'm not saying you can't do them. Nothing is written in stone. There are always exceptions.

On to the third tool which is your friend and can help you create deep point of view.

This tool stems from a concept that I learned in my graduate training in psychology called the fundamental attribution error. The fundamental attribution error is a psychological phenomenon in which a person (actor) and an observer attribute the person's (actor's) actions differently from one another. Those attributions differ in a very specific way, which we'll describe below. This is a useful tool when writing fiction. It will help you reveal the internal life of your point of view characters. We'll illustrate what we mean in a moment.

This attribution error is especially true of negative acts and emotions. People will almost always deny that they were angry, jealous, or aggressive, but will often justify their actions by referring to the bad behavior of others.

Imagine that Joe and Sally are in a bar. Another man approaches and starts talking to Sally. Joe punches the second man in the face. Why did he do that?

Joe, here, is our actor. The bartender is an observer. He's standing behind the bar watching all this.

If you ask the bartender why Joe hit the other man, he may say, "Joe's an aggressive and jealous guy, especially when he gets a few drinks in him." The bartender will look to Joe's personality for an explanation.

If you ask Joe, he'll say, "That bastard was hitting on my woman!" Joe will look to the situation at hand for an explanation.

In other words, the bartender (the observer) will attribute Joe's aggression to something inside Joe, while Joe (the actor) will attribute his aggression to something in his environment.

Remember: People will almost always deny that they were angry, jealous, or aggressive. Instead, they will justify their actions by referring to the bad behavior of others.

In another example, imagine an angry woman. She's scowling and has clenched one hand into a fist.

If you ask her, "Why are you so mad?" she may say something like, "I'm not mad. If he wants to make a fool of himself in front of his boss, that's his problem." We, as observers, attribute her actions to something inside her— her anger. She, on the other hand, will blame her actions on the bad behavior of the man she mentions, perhaps her husband, who she believes is making a fool of himself in front of his boss.

We generally won't admit when we're angry. Instead, we point to something outside ourselves to justify our behavior.

If we're pushed, we may admit it and say, "Yeah, yeah, okay. I'm angry." But if Beth is in the car with me on the freeway, and she says, "Alice, why are you so angry?" I'm going to say, "That idiot cut me off." I'm not going to talk about why I'm angry. I might even object. "I'm not being angry. I'm being perfectly rational, because that idiot cut me off."

Generally, when people make attributions about their own feelings and behaviors and thoughts, they will look for an explanation for how they feel, or think, or behave, in the external world around them.

So, how can we use this in our writing?

EXAMPLE: SHE'S SHY

LET'S say we have someone who's fearful and socially awkward, like our Carla in the other scene, and she's in a social situation. Maybe she's standing in the corner. If you asked her, "What's going on with you?," she's not going to say, "Well, you know, I'm really very shy, and this kind of scares me." She's more likely to look at the people around her and say they'd all make fun of her if she uttered a word. She's going to use an explanation for what's in the external world to explain her own feelings.

EXAMPLE: HE'S JEALOUS

IN THE ABOVE EXAMPLE, how would Joe explain why he behaved as he did? He probably wouldn't say, "I'm a jealous guy." He'd probably say something like: "That bastard was looking down the front of her dress."

I actually got this jealousy scene out of the book, *Seize the Fire*, by Laura Kinsale. The hero and heroine were sitting at the lunch table with another man, who, as I recall, had been engaged to the heroine. We're in the hero's point of view.

He's watching the heroine with the former fiancé and notes to himself, "He's looking down the front of her dress."

To me, as a reader, I'm looking at that and thinking, "Well, maybe he's looking down the front of her dress, but the important thing is, the hero is jealous. Isn't that cute?" But that's not what's going on in his head. He's looking to the outside world, blaming his feelings on another person's action.

EXAMPLE: HE'S ANGRY

YOU COULD RESTATE THAT AS: "I'm not angry. The morons didn't know what they were talking about."

EXAMPLE: SHE'S HAPPY

RESTATED AS: "Hallelujah! The prize committee awarded the blue ribbon to the rose she'd slaved over for years. All her hours and hours of work had paid off, and now her nursery would flourish."

Another example: Someone might say, "Alice, you're very happy."

I'm not likely to tell them, "Well, I'm generally a happy person," even though I am. What I'm going to say to them is, "You bet I'm happy. I just got a three-book contract." I'm going to talk about what's going on in the outside world.

EXAMPLE: HE'S CYNICAL

SOMEONE WHO'S cynical is not likely to admit they're cynical. They're more likely to think, "The world sucked, and if you stuck your neck out to help someone, they'd likely bite you on the ass," including all the mixed metaphors in there. You're not going to admit you're cynical. You're going to say, *"There's a problem with the world, and I'm onto it."*

EXAMPLE: SHE WAS CAREFREE

She was carefree and probably unrealistic.
Perhaps cruising for a fall.

THIS COULD BE RESTATED AS: Why worry about such things? They always worked out for the best in the end.

PEOPLE ARE NATURAL PSYCHOLOGISTS

People love to discover insights into other people. It makes them feel clever. For example, when I was reading the Laura Kinsale book and I came across that little passage I mentioned above. "Oh, Sheridan's jealous. Isn't that cute?" I felt clever. I discovered something that probably Sheridan wasn't even aware of and it gave me an A-ha! feeling. You've probably experienced this too. It gives you a feeling that you've discovered something, and you get a little zing of pleasure from that discovery.

When you can work these attribution differences into your stories, you'll be able to reveal the internal workings of your point of view character. You'll also give your reader a pleasurable experience, since they'll feel clever, being natural psychologist, as they discover what's really happening to your point of view character.

TO RECAP

We went through our three sets of tools—three types of verbs and internal monologue—neither of which are your friends—and the fundamental attribution error that is your friend.

With this third tool, you can use it by having

your point of view character explain their own motivations, feelings, and actions through attributing them to the outside world. This tool can make your writing rich and insert you deeply in the person's point of view. Now, let's move to the exceptions.

Part 2

Exceptions
───────────

EXCEPTION #1:

THE BEGINNING OF A SCENE/STORY

WHEN YOU'RE at the very beginning of a scene, you want to set the point of view quickly and may need to use one of the verbs that aren't your friends, like a perceiving verb in the example below. Otherwise, the reader could be confused, thinking she's in one point of view and then a couple of paragraphs later, she finds out that, no, this is somebody else's point of view.

EXAMPLE
Susie saw the rider approach.

This sentence tells you immediately we're in Susie's head. We know we're looking at the world out of Susie's eyes and experiencing it through her emotions. That's a good time to actually use one of those telling verbs.

EXCEPTION #2:

TO AVOID CONFUSION

You've read my book and you encounter some of these phrases in your work: *"she thought," "she saw," "she wanted,"* or *"she hoped."* Then you think, "Well, I should really try to rewrite that." You try and try, and twist yourself and the reader into knots, ending up with German word order. It's just a pain in the neck. They'd have to diagram your sentence to understand what it is you're talking about. Don't do it. Just go ahead and use one of those verbs anyway. Just try not to use them too much.

EXCEPTION #3:

SHORT, EMOTIONAL, INTERNAL OUTBURSTS

When you want to occasionally portray short, emotional outbursts, internal monologue is appropriate.

After I wrote about this exception, I noticed there was internal monologue in the book I was writing. I looked at it and I looked at it, and thought, "I actually like this."

In this example, a historical romance, we're in Anna's point of view. Peter and Anna are about to make love for the first time. Peter does not know that Anna isn't a virgin, and Anna knows that he's going to be very disappointed in her when he finds out if she doesn't tell him first She's trying to make herself tell him.

AN EXAMPLE OF AN EXCEPTION USING INTERNAL MONOLOGUE

"Peter," she managed to whisper.

"Yes, my love. Anything." He kissed her throat again—that sensitive spot just under her ear. How had he made that inch of flesh so responsive to his touch?

"I have to tell you something."

"It can wait." He had her out of her corset now, and it joined her dress in a heap on the floor. Nothing but her shift stood between her body and his view, his touch. She had to speak now, before she was naked.

"Please, it's important."

He stopped undressing her, although he kept his hands on her shoulders. "Why now, Anna?"

"It could affect the way you feel about me." *Tell him, damn it. Tell him.*

"Nothing could do that."

"It's just that I—"

He cupped her chin and kissed her briefly. Sweetly. "You're nervous, of course. Don't worry. I'll be gentle."

"Not that." *Tell him!*

He stood, waiting, gazing into her eyes with such adoration on his face. What would she do if he turned and left? How could she face herself or their friends? What if he hated her?

AS AN ASIDE, I'll submit that those last three sentences are a pretty good representation of what goes through someone's head when she's afraid of rejection.

I broke my own rule. I certainly could have just turned it into third-person past tense.

"It could affect the way you feel about me." She had to tell him, dammit. She really did."

I like what I originally did better, so I decided to keep it. I'll tell you what I absolutely would not do. I wouldn't write: "*Tell him, dammit*, she thought. *Tell him*." That would definitely tell me this was the author talking. This is an intimate, important scene. You don't want any author intrusion yanking the reader out of the story.

I break my own rules, and you can break my rules too. They're not rules anyway, just tools to help you create deep point of view.

Take what's useful and leave the rest.

SO, what's my advice?

As you write and revise, be aware of the language areas that aren't your friends.

- Sensing Verbs
- Thinking Verbs
- Emoting Verbs
- Internal Monologue

See if there's a better, more intimate way to convey them by showing in detail rather than telling.

And, look for places where you can use the fundamental attribution error to convey your point of view character's internal thoughts and feelings. This last tool is your friend.

I like to write fairly clean first drafts and try

to fix these things as I go along, but it makes equally good sense to use this advice when you edit.

If you're someone who likes to put down words and then come back and fix them, I don't want to trip you up so you're stopping when you shouldn't be stopping. Go ahead and write out all your words, but when you come back to edit and rewrite, look for these things, and spend a little time. It doesn't take that long. Sometimes it's just taking out "she wondered" or "she thought," and see if there's a better way to write them.

Look for places where you can use the fundamental attribution error to convey your point of view character's internal thoughts and feelings, especially by projecting them onto the environment. "I'm not angry. He's being an idiot," for example.

As you write or edit, see if you can implement these tools. See if they help you. If they don't, don't use them. Write your own way, but my very long experience tells me these deep point of view tools can be very helpful to you.

Happy Writing!

Q&A

Q: How does this work with first person?

A: Pretty much the same. For example, you wouldn't write: "I thought he was attractive." Write instead: "He was attractive."

Q: For deep POV, there are verbs (thought, saw, etc.) that should be eliminated. Are there cases where they're really needed? e.g. If an enemy who was invisible suddenly became visible: "She saw him coming right at her."

A: You don't need "She saw," in there. "He suddenly became visible," or, "The enemy appeared on the hilltop, and he was coming right at her," would work. Or, "The monster suddenly showed up, blood dripping from his fangs, and he was coming right at her." Or, "He suddenly became visible."

Q: What's the difference between deep point of view and other points of view?

A: Deep point of view allows readers to be more intimately involved with the character. It puts them inside the main character's head. Readers experience things as the POV person experiences them. There's lots of different kinds of point of view, including first person, second person, third person, and omniscient. Except for omniscient, you can use the tools I describe here when writing in first- or second- person. All the examples in this book are in third-person.

To answer the question, Deep point of view creates intimacy. The reader is directly inside the point of view character's head and experiences things as the character experiences them. Some people call this third-person limited.

Q: Could you recommend any novels that are written totally in deep point of view?

A: (Editor's reply) *Bridget Jones' Diary*, books by Nora Roberts, Suzanne Brockmann, Alice Gaines, J.R. Ward, Nalini Singh, and Karen Marie Moning.

Q: How often "should" the POV switch in a scene/chapter in order to still provide clarity?

A: For a point of view purist like me, the point of view shouldn't switch in a scene. You never *have to* switch. You can do an entire book in one point of view if you want. There's never a requirement that you switch point of view. In the beginning of the book, I discussed switching point of view within a scene. It's certainly done, and it can be done well, but you don't want to do it too often, maybe once or twice within a scene. I prefer just to stay in one point of view for an entire scene. Now, a chapter has several scenes in it. As many scenes as there are, you can have different points of view within a chapter. Again, nothing is written in stone. There's no *should*.

Q: When writing in a hero/heroine's POV, how do you add their description so the reader knows what the character's look like without popping out and having the author intrusion?

A: This sounds like a romance question. Assuming you're using both points of view in the book, have the hero describe the heroine, and have the heroine describe the hero. It's just the easiest way to do it. The old thing of somebody looking in a mirror and describing themselves to themselves is contrived, and part of the problem. Even if we're totally beautiful, and we have the most beautiful eyes in the world, or we have the most beautiful hair in the world, or the whitest teeth in the world, when you look in the mirror, you don't generally think, "Oh, look at how white my teeth are. Look at how beautiful my eyes are." They're your eyes. You look at them every day. You'll notice if your eyes are red or puffy. You worry, maybe, about what kind of hair day you're going to have, but you don't generally look at yourself in the mirror, "Look at my long, blonde hair, and my blue eyes."

In *Flowers from the Storm* by Laura Kinsale, there's a scene where the hero and heroine are together with the heroine's father in the same room. The heroine's father is blind and asks the hero to describe the heroine to him, and he does it in such amazing detail. If you can think up something like that, very clever. If you're only in one point of view for the entire book, you could have the other person comment on your point of view character's appearance.

Q: How deep do you go without boring the reader with too much and not enough action? Do you have to break it out by how big the book is in page count?

A: Whether writing a short story or a full-length novel, I'd use the techniques shared in this book. In the examples, deep point of view occurs via both action and dialogue. You don't stop for paragraphs of the POV character's thoughts. As long as you're writing to entertain, balancing the character's emotional inner workings with action and dialogue, utilizing these techniques of deep point of view will not bore your reader. It will produce the opposite result because it will help your reader identify with the main character in such a way that they won't want to put the book down.

Q: How do you stop yourself from slipping into "telling" instead of "showing"?

A: Verbs. Those verbs. That is the simplest way. I would suggest you use the cheat sheet here: http://bethb.net/deeppovbook—the perceiving verbs, thinking verbs, and the emoting verbs—and have that in front of you as you're writing or editing. If you don't use those verbs that get in the way of deep point of view, you can definitely keep yourself from slipping from showing into telling.

Q: How much is too much when describing a scene/how a character feels?

A: That's an interesting question. We're probably all aware of information dumps and long descriptions. You always need to have something going on in your story. You can have short scenes where the character is licking his wounds and not much occurs, but where he's recovering from something awful that just happened and is now girding up for the next battle. In general, what I would look for, if I'm concerned there's too much description or introspection, are long paragraphs, because that's where too much description is likely to happen. If you find long paragraphs, you may not be able to fix them just by adding a hard return and starting a new paragraph. Those might be places where there's just too much description, or too much introspection.

Certainly, description is best done in little bits. When the hero meets the heroine, for example, you don't want him noticing her eye color, the fit of her dress, hair color and style, all in the same paragraph.

Instead, the first thing he can notice is her smile. Then later on, he can notice a bit more:

"Oh, and look, she has beautiful blue eyes." As she turns to walk away, he can notice more: "Yeah, she's got a really good derriere too." Drop it in in bits. Don't over-describe. It's useful to leave a little to the reader's imagination. For a secondary character who isn't very important, you don't have to tell what they look like at all. Just let the reader figure out what the person looks like by what they say and do.

Q: How do you use deep POV but maintain the voice of a narrator in your story?

A: The point of view character is your narrator. Now, I know we all want to be beautiful writers, and we all do have our own voice. There's no way you can take your own voice out of the story. There just simply isn't. All those characters, they're you. You're producing them. If you want to use deep point of view—you don't always have to—the narrator is the point of view character. Don't worry that you're going to lose your voice. Your voice is always going to be in there. You and I can use exactly the same examples. We can write exactly the same scenes, and we will write them completely differently. Don't worry about that. Just make the character the narrator of the story.

Q: I was wondering if you could talk a little about when to use deep POV and when not to. Would you avoid deep POV with a character who is evil, insane, or otherwise not easy to empathize with?

A: There are examples when you wouldn't want to use deep point of view. One thing Alicia Rasley said in her book, *The Power of Point of View*, that absolutely blew my mind: "If you have a character who's about to be executed in the next hour or so, you might not want to be in that person's point of view at all, period. But I certainly think you don't want to be in deep point of view about it. I don't even know how you could convey that sort of thing. I can't ask anyone who was ever executed what it felt like. I don't want to feel like that.

If you have a John Proctor—a character from a play, not a book—who's about to be hanged for witchcraft, and you have a scene between him and his wife Elizabeth right before he's hanged, you might not want to be in John's point of view. You might want to be in Elizabeth's instead.

Deep point of view might be difficult to do in a situation that's just absolutely horrible.

The second part of the question: "Would you avoid deep point of view with a character who's evil?" Not necessarily. In a book I recently turned into my editor, I have a secondary character who is the evil stepmother. It's contemporary, not a fairy tale. She's the stepmother of the heroine, and she's not a nice person. She's a bad person. I didn't give her a point of view, but had I done it, I would still get deeply into her point of view. The stepmother really did not like Nicole from the time they met. The two of them just did not get along. She referred to Nicole as a brat, and tried to convince Nicole's father to have her sent away to boarding school.

That's how Nicole views her, of course. If I try to get into the stepmother's point of view, I'm now in her world view. In the stepmother's view, Nicole *is* a brat. There probably are things in her memory, in her experiences with Nicole that make her feel this way. Perhaps she blames Nicole for the loss of her marriage. I can justify the stepmother's point of view. It is a perfectly reasonable thing for her to say or think: "I hate that little brat. I'm going to get her." Now, that doesn't mean she's sympathetic. She's not, and no reader is going to be fooled into thinking she's a good person, but you can still create some kind of empathy that allows you to get into her point of view.

If you're going to write about someone who's insane, you'd better understand what it means to be insane. It's not the evil character who's going to conquer the world, *bwahaha*.

Insane is probably someone who's psychotic or perhaps someone who is manic-depressive. They're having crazy ideas going through their heads all the time. They're probably not living in the real world. A psychotic person usually has a break with reality. If they're schizophrenic, they often have auditory hallucinations.

You can empathize, not sympathize, with evil characters. If you want to use deep point of view, put yourself in their head. And when you do, you'll discover that they have a perfectly valid reason to their way of thinking for everything they do and feel.

Q: Is it wise to use two POV's in a story, i.e., switching between first person and omniscient from chapter to chapter?

A: Those are two different questions. Of course, you can use two points of view in one story, and in romance, we routinely do. We have the hero and the heroine. Now, switching between first-person and omniscient... You've got a little problem there, because first-person is the most intimate there is, and omniscient is least intimate. That's interesting, but what I'm really worried about is how this will be carried out from chapter to chapter. If you're constantly going back and forth, you might have a valid reason for doing that. However, if you're writing romance, you may have a hard time finding a publisher.

Q: How do I best write necessary descriptions or more informational bits so they are consistent with the deep POV of my heroine?

A: You write it from their point of view, from their world view. When you start writing, you learn examples, such as what does a sunny day mean? For someone who's been in a cabin in the wilderness during a dreadful winter, and now it's getting to be warm, and the sun is coming out, the snow is melting, and the crocuses are starting to bloom, they'd say, "That's wonderful. Isn't it great?" How about someone who's been in the desert for a couple of days and hasn't had anything to drink? They'd say or think, "Another sunny day. Oh my God." Everything is perceived through the point of view character.

Q: I have heard people say that deep POV can be too stressful for some readers who do not want to feel so close to the protagonist. However, I think that makes the reading experience more exciting. What do you think?

A: Obviously, I love deep point of view. That's why I'm writing this book. Earlier we discussed writing in the point of view of someone who is about to be executed. To be in the point of view of someone who constantly relives the commission of a vicious crime might overwhelm the reader. I've never experienced those things.

If someone told me they found something they read too stressful, I'd ask about what they were reading and want to know what they found so stressful. In romance, because of the happy ending—the thing that everybody puts us down for—we're allowed to put our characters through absolute torture because the reader knows everything will be fixed in the end.

The characters can go through very stressful times. If they don't, you might not be writing romance, but definitely, the stressful times makes the romance more exciting and more intimate.

Q: If you use internal monologue, would you write it in italics or not? And why would you italicize some, if any?

A: If I were going to use it, I'd put it in italics, but I recommend not using it. As mentioned in my exceptions to the rule above, you may want to italicize short, emotional outbursts, as is my example in the exceptions above. That was basically my heroine yelling at herself.

Editor note: This "self as the self's own audience" is what necessitates the italics. All of the other internal monologue is just a direct window into the thoughts going through her head, but when she silently yells at herself, these commands are best treated almost like they are directed at an "other."

Q: If you're writing primarily, maybe even exclusively, in deep point of view, when might you want to pull back out of deep point of view, besides the exceptions shared in this book?

A: Perhaps when you're writing about something that's extremely stressful, like someone who's about to be executed.

Editor's reply: The mystery author Michael Connelly writes from a distant or removed third-person point of view most of the time. Every once in a while, Connelly dips into deep point of view, the reverse of what we do in romance. I think it works because his main character, Hieronymus Bosch, a homicide detective, has to distance himself from his work, most of the time, and this necessitates a limited use of deep point of view. That's another example of how someone makes valid use of what can be called distant or shallow third-person point of view.

Next Steps and Bonuses

Because You Have Read This Book

SIGN UP FOR CHECKLISTS, handouts, and bonuses, including a 50% off coupon to the live course this book is adapted from here:

http://bethb.net/deeppovbook

Resources

CHRISTOU, Rhay, (2014) from the blog Writers in the Storm,

    http://writersinthestormblog.-com/2014/10/diving-deep-into-deep-point of view/

ELAINE, Kelly, (2012) The Beginning Writer "Different Types of Point of View,"

    http://www.thebeginningwriter.com/2012/03/look-at-different-types-of-point-of.html

ELDREDGE, Genevieve Iseult (2018),

    http://angeledits.blogspot.com/2016/02/top-10-reasons-editors-reject-erotic.html

GAINES, Alice. (2018) Barany School of Fiction, "Mastering Deep Point of View with Alice Gains, A Training,"

https://school.bethbarany.com/p/mastering-deep-point of view-with-alice-gaines

GAINES, Alice, et al (2014) "Getting the Author off the Page," *Writing Romance: The Ultimate Guide on Craft, Creation and Industry Connections*, SFA-RWA Publishing

HILL, Beth, (2016) The Editor's Blog, Deep Point of View: What's So Deep About it?,

http://theeditorsblog.net/2011/11/16/deep-pov-whats-so-deep-about-it/

KIEFFER, Kristen (2015) How to Write in Deep Point of View,

https://www.well-storied.com/blog/how-to-write-in-deep-pov

KINSALE, Laura, (2014) *Seize the Fire*, Open Road Media Romance

KINSALE, Laura (2003) *Flowers from the Storm*, Harper Collins

RASLEY, Alicia, (2008) *The Power of Point of View: Make Your Story Come to Life*, Writer's Digest Books

About the Author

Alice Gaines is a *USA Today* best-selling author who writes about nice people having outrageous sex. She's published in numerous houses, including Red Sage, Dorchester, Harlequin Spice Briefs, Carina Press, and Avon Impulse. Her Regency romance, *Captain and Countess*, was one of the first ten books selected for Kindle Scout. Over her long career, she's won several awards and contests for her writing. She currently writes erotic contemporary romance and sizzling paranormal romance for Entangled Publishing and Changeling Press. With a PhD in Psychology from UC Berkeley, she is a firm believer that deep point of view is a powerful tool for pulling readers into your story.

If you have questions or would just like to say hi, you can write to Alice at authoralice-gaines@gmail.com. Visit her site here: http://alicegaines.blogspot.com/. If you'd like to sign up for her mailing list, go to: http://eepurl.com/boeGm9. From time to time, she raffles off her knitting and crocheting projects to someone on her list.

48048022R10050

Made in the USA
Columbia, SC
06 January 2019